Choose

"These books a... the choice seem... like it will solve every-thing, but you wonder if it's a trap."

Matt Harmon, age 11

"I think you'd call this a book for active readers, and I am definitely an active reader!"

Ava Kendrick, age 11

"You decide your own fate, but your fate is still a surprise."

Chun Tao Lin, age 10

"Come on in this book if you're crazy enough! One wrong move and you're a goner!"

Ben Curley, age 9

"You can read *Choose Your Own Adventure* books so many wonderful ways. You could go find your dog or follow a unicorn."

Celia Lawton, 11

CHOOSE YOUR OWN ADVENTURE®

NIGHTMARE

BLOOD ISLAND

BY LIZ WINDOVER

ILLUSTRATED BY GABHOR UTOMO

CHOOSECO

WAITSFIELD, VERMONT

Illustrated by: Gabhor Utomo
Book design: Stacey Boyd, Big Eyedea Visual Design

For information regarding permission, write to:

CHOOSECO

P.O. Box 46
Waitsfield, Vermont 05673
www.cyoa.com

ISBN 10 1-937133-46-X
ISBN 13 978-1-937133-46-7

Published simultaneously in the United States and Canada

Printed in Canada

9 8 7 6 5 4 3 2 1

To my parents,
for their endless encouragement.

BEWARE and WARNING!

This book is different from other books.

You and YOU ALONE are in charge of what happens in this story.

There are dangers, choices, adventures, and consequences. YOU must use all of your wits to stay out of trouble. The wrong decision could end in disaster—even death. But, don't despair. At any time, YOU can go back and make another choice, alter the path of your story, and change its result.

You are about to embark on your dream assignment. You will join several young biologists and researchers aboard the Albatross III, in search of a rumored species never before documented by humans: the crested adzebill. If you can bring back proof of this prehistoric bird's current existence, you'll be famous! But you will need enormous courage to scour the adzebill's supposed home. Nicknamed Blood Island, this remote Pacific outpost is plagued by eerie rumors. Visitors to the island rarely speak of it, if they do return. First you must survive a violent storm and difficult sea voyage—and from there, it will only get tougher. Good luck!

You grip the cool, white railing at the stern of *Albatross III*, the ship where you'll be living for the next three weeks. The gleaming boat pulls away from the dock with a honk of her horn, and you take a deep breath to settle your nerves.

You are leading a team of research scientists on a trip to investigate a species of giant flightless bird—the crested adzebill—which was once presumed extinct. It will take five days to sail from San Francisco to a remote island in the Pacific Ocean where the adzebill was recently sighted. You're nearly finished with your degree in zoology, and if you can find the bird, the discovery could make your career. There are eleven other young scientists with you from the university, plus ten crew members.

Turn to the next page.

2

As the ship makes a wide turn and glides smoothly beneath the Golden Gate Bridge, you see your friend Andrea come up from below deck.

"Andrea, hey!" you wave. "I wondered where you were hiding."

"Had to scope out the ship first!" she says. Andrea is another student in your department studying extinct species of the Pacific Islands.

"Were you able to find out why our destination is called Blood Island?" you ask.

"Not yet," Andrea says. "All I know is we'll be there in five days! I'm so excited. Can you believe it? We could be the ones to prove that the adzebill isn't extinct after all!"

"I know," you say, grinning. "It would be great. But I still don't understand how the adzebill—a prehistoric species—could be living on an island that formed from a volcano so recently."

"Well," Andrea says, "that's what the geologists say. But I'm not so sure. I think it's just an excuse for why no one's discovered the island before now."

"I guess we'll find out in five days, huh?" you say, turning to look across the ocean stretching endlessly in front of you.

Turn to page 4.

4

Four days later, after dinner, you're sitting in the dining cabin with Andrea reading about *moa-nalo,* giant extinct ducks, in your brand-new copy of *A Photographic Field Guide to Hawaii's Most Exotic Birds*. The atmosphere in the cabin is rowdy and warm. You're supposed to reach land tomorrow, and people are getting excited.

"Can you believe Glen beat me at chess again today?" Andrea laments, glaring at Glen across the room. "I used to think I was pretty good."

You look up from your book just in time to see Glen put Natasha into checkmate, eliciting a round of whoops and cheers. Then, out of the kitchen, comes Mak, one of the ship's cooks. The two of you have become friends over the past few days—he's a little older than you and grew up in Hawaii.

"What's up, Mak?" you ask.

"You wanted to know more about Blood Island?" Mak asks.

Cooper, the other kitchen guy, has followed Mak over to your table.

"Ask Ernie," Cooper says. "He knows."

Go on to the next page.

Ernie is one of the deckhands. He's so weather-beaten, he looks about 90 years old. He's sitting at the next table. At Cooper's words, he turns his kindly face toward you.

"Blood Island is cursed," he says quietly, and turns back to his dinner.

A few of the others in the room have stopped what they were doing and are listening in.

"Yeah, but what do you mean, 'cursed'?" Mak says. "Curses aren't real."

"Oh, this one is," Ernie says, matter-of-factly. "A lot of people died there a long, long time ago. The people who settled the island, and sailors too. No one really knows how, because no one has ever lived to tell the tale." Ernie takes another bite of beef stew. "But I've seen things…it's not called Blood Island for nothing."

"What did you see?" asks Glen, who has moved closer to hear the conversation. "You know," he announces, "I heard that the last research team—the ones that reported seeing the adzebill—they're all in a psychiatric ward now."

Ernie doesn't look up from his bowl. He shrugs his shoulders and nods his head, but doesn't say anything further.

"Well, believe what you want," Cooper interjects. "I know you all have work to do out there, but I'm not setting foot off this boat."

You and Andrea and Mak exchange glances. As a scientist, you form your opinions based on facts, not rumors. And you certainly do not believe in curses.

Still, Ernie's story leaves you feeling uneasy.

Turn to the next page.

6

That night, sleep comes slowly. You finally drift off with the rocking of the boat.

The next thing you know, you hear a thunderous BANG! and you're thrown from your bed. What was that?! You run up on deck. The wind is whipping and the waves are roaring. Through the ship's bright lights, you see rain coming down in thick sheets.

"Get back inside!" someone shouts. It's Andrea and Mak. They are behind you, holding onto the door frame and squinting against the blowing rain.

The ship begins listing to one side. You must be taking on water. Then you look overboard into the waves and see an enormous whirlpool right next to the ship! It's a few hundred feet across and spinning with a violent force. The center goes so deep that you can't see the bottom.

A huge wave slams the deck, soaking all three of you to your skin. You've got both arms wrapped around the railing, but you still almost lose your grip. You look into the whirlpool. The spinning, swirling, roiling green-black water is hypnotic. You realize with a lurch of your stomach that *Albatross III* is getting closer to the vortex. You might be past the point of no return.

Turn to page 8.

8

The ship keeps tilting, keeps picking up speed, until you're nearly sideways against the vortex's inner wall. Your body is pressed against the deck from the centrifugal force. The wind shrieks, like a chorus of people screaming for help. Or is that actually a chorus of people screaming for help? You can't think straight. The pressure of the spin becomes too great. Your eyes roll back in your head. The world dissolves into a gray vacuum, then into a silent black hole.

You awake with a mighty cough, spewing out seawater. You blink your eyes open and see a sky smudgy with dark gray clouds. Your head is pounding in pain, and your arms are weak. You manage to sit up. You're on a long, wide beach bordered by jungle. A lumpy, lush mountain, shrouded in spectral mist, towers beyond the tree line. Its top is obscured by clouds. The whole scene is dark. Even the sand beneath your feet is dark gray, almost black. You wonder if it's volcanic.

You look at your watch, a cheap digital one you bought just for the trip. You're surprised to see the seconds still ticking by dutifully. But the time says 1:37 AM. This is impossible given the fact that there's light in the sky right now.

You wipe your forehead and see blood smeared on your hand. At a loud clattering sound, you whirl around to see the remnants of *Albatross III* strewn across the sand—and Andrea emerging from the wreckage!

Go on to the next page.

"Andrea! Are you okay? What happened?"

Andrea stumbles over some debris toward you. "Yes, I'm fine." Her shirt sleeve is badly torn and her lip is cut.

"What happened?" you ask again. "I think I passed out…"

"Me too," she said. "Last thing I remember is being sucked into that hole in the ocean…" She gestures helplessly behind her at the ruined ship. It's lying on its side. The hull is cracked in two. Random shafts of splintered wood and metal lay here and there.

"Where is everyone else?" you ask, afraid of the answer.

Andrea grimaces and shakes her head but doesn't meet your eyes.

You both begin to walk the perimeter of the wreck, and as you come around the other side, you hear a loud groan and see the bulky shape of Mak struggling out from underneath a piece of metal sheeting. He looks disoriented. His eyes focus in and out on your face before he sighs deeply and stumbles over to grab you both in a big hug of relief.

"Hey, look!" Andrea says looking over Mak's shoulder when he lets go. She lifts a piece of the wreckage, revealing a bright red canvas bag. Mak drags it to the beach and opens it up. It's an emergency kit containing thirty or forty energy bars, some flare guns, a couple of two-way radios, a compass, matches, and a flashlight. You realize you're starving, so you all grab a few energy bars and sit down to eat them on the sand.

Turn to the next page.

10

"What should we do?" you say. "It's getting dark, it must be evening."

Your energy bar tastes like weirdly flavored cardboard.

"We should find water..." Andrea says, absent-mindedly pouring a handful of sand onto her feet.

"Gotta find someplace to sleep..." Mak adds. He's looking out at the ocean as if he'll find the answers there.

You keep getting a weird feeling, like someone is watching you. Your scalp prickles, and your body has this jumpy feeling of anticipation. You look over your shoulder, again, at the dark jungle, but you don't see anyone or anything. Just a thick wall of leaves and vines. The island is supposed to be uninhabited, but still...

Andrea finishes her energy bar and stands up. "I really think water should be priority number one," she says. "We're all dehydrated, I'm sure of it."

"I'm definitely not going into those trees right now, not if it's getting dark," Mak announces, shaking his head.

Andrea sighs and looks at you. "What do you think we should do?"

*If you decide to build a shelter first,
turn to page 13.*

*If you decide to find water first,
turn to page 52.*

"I think we should turn back," you say. "That storm looks serious."

Mak and Andrea reluctantly agree. You turn the raft around and begin paddling back to shore. The clouds take over, and a cold wind picks up.

"We'd better hurry, or we're going to get caught in it anyway," Andrea says, looking behind you. "It's moving a lot faster than we are."

As you get closer to shore, a bank of mist passes over the beach. When it clears, you see the horrible vision from your dream: human heads on stakes all along the beach, with blood red sand underneath. They seem to be a warning not to set foot on the island.

"What the—" Mak exclaims. He is staring at the beach, having just noticed the heads. "It's just like my dream...it's real..." he says in horror.

You look behind you again, and the storm has rolled in completely, covering the whole sky at your back. Lightning flashes nonstop, and the water is choppy and white-capped.

Turn to page 23.

Andrea pulls a five gallon bucket out of the wreckage on the beach. You would have used it for collecting scientific samples if everything had gone according to plan.

"Okay, well, I can only bring so much water back by myself," she snaps, walking into the trees. "See you soon."

"What if she gets lost?" you ask Mak.

"She'll be fine," Mak answers. "Help me with the shelter, would you?"

Before long, you've managed to prop together several large pieces of wreckage into a makeshift lean-to. Andrea has not returned. You keep glancing out at the horizon, hoping that you'll see a ship coming to your rescue, but none appear.

You get a prickly feeling down your neck like someone is watching you. You turn back toward the jungle, but nothing is there. You take a deep breath and shake your head.

Turn to the next page.

14

An hour later, you and Mak sit by a small fire, watching the stars. The sun has set and the clouds have dispersed, but the air is still heavy with tropical warmth. Andrea has not returned.

"Think she's okay, Mak?" you ask.

"I hope so," he says. "Maybe we should have gone with her after all."

He looks genuinely worried now, which you didn't expect.

If you decide to stay up to wait for Andrea, go on to the next page.

If you decide you should try to get some sleep, turn to page 42.

You are exhausted, but you will yourself to stay awake. Mak falls asleep in front of the fire next to you, and then you start to nod off.

Andrea shakes you awake sometime later. You can hardly see her by the light of the dying fire.

"Andrea! We were getting worried," you say, sitting up. "What took so long? Did you get lost?"

"I found water." Andrea says quietly and points to the full bucket. She looks oddly calm.

You stumble over to the bucket and scoop handful after handful of cold, fresh water into your parched mouth. You feel guilty that you didn't go with her.

"Are you okay?" you ask.

She raises her eyebrows. "I'm fine," she says lightly, as if she had only been gone for five minutes. Then she heads into the lean-to. You rouse Mak, and you both join her in the shelter. The three of you immediately fall asleep.

Turn to the next page.

16

In the safety of the lean-to, you enter a deep sleep and dream you are wandering a foggy landscape—part jungle, part endless beach. You're searching for someone. The fog rolls away from the sand, revealing tall stakes stuck into the ground. There is a human head jammed onto each stake. They look like they are still alive. You know they can't be, but the eyes and lips are moving. You want to turn and run, but suddenly your feet are stuck in the sand like concrete.

The sand below the stakes turns crimson with dripping blood. The breaking waves turn into a pinkish-green foam. You look behind you and call out for Mak and Andrea—they emerge from the lean-to, but their heads are missing. You're slammed with nausea, and then everything starts shaking.

Mak is shaking you awake. It's morning.

Turn to the next page.

18

"Wake up! You'll never guess what we found!" Mak says eagerly.

You sit up and recall your horrible dream. It's another dark, cloudy day. The mountaintop is still lost in clouds. Even though you were dreaming, you feel like you saw something real that happened long ago.

"Nightmare? We had them too," Mak says with a shudder. "But hey, we found a raft!"

"A raft?" you ask in amazement and follow their gaze across the beach to an oblong white capsule about the size of an oil drum.

"It inflates when you pull the cord out," Mak says with excitement.

"Relatively speaking, we're not far from Hawaii," Andrea says. "It might be worth a shot. The currents should bring us close enough to the shipping lane at the very least."

You feel an instant surge of hope and relief, but looking out at the empty ocean, you're also worried. What if you get lost, or another storm hits and the raft capsizes?

Go on to the next page.

"If we could reach Hawaii or a ship we'd be saved," you say. "But isn't it dangerous?"

"It might not be as bad as you think," Mak says thoughtfully. "Life rafts are really high-tech these days—they're designed to hold a lot of people afloat for a long time. It will even have a roof when it inflates. Another storm could do us in, but hopefully we would reach safety first."

"I was thinking about exploring the island more before we decide," Andrea says. "Maybe that shipwreck way down the beach?"

You follow Andrea's pointing finger. You see part of a wrecked ship, with broken masts and drooping sails. You wonder how old it is and whether there might be anything useful or interesting on board.

If you think it's best to set out in the raft now, before wasting any more time, turn to page 20.

If you're hesitant to venture out on the water and would prefer to explore the shipwreck first, turn to page 25.

20

"Let's go find Hawaii!" you say, putting on a brave face. "It isn't any safer here without good supplies."

The three of you drag the rescue raft down the beach toward the water, and Mak yanks the cord hard. It opens with a pop, and the orange and black rubber billows quickly into a square raft, big enough for about 4 or 5 people. It even has a tented roof, just like Mak said it would. The best part, which makes your heart lift a little bit, is the emergency kit stashed in a side pocket: more flares, an air pump, a signal mirror, waterproof flashlight, a rescue ring, paddles, patch kit, and whistle.

You gather the other supplies and what's left of the water Andrea found. Mak said the roof on the raft not only protects you from the sun but will also collect rain water. You hope he knows what he's talking about.

Go on to the next page.

You break out of the clouds and fog around the island into the open sea. The sun beats down on you. The roof on the raft shields you from getting a sunburn, but it feels like a greenhouse underneath.

You take a turn holding the compass while Mak and Andrea row. As they paddle, you glance back at the island growing smaller behind you against a bigger and bigger sky.

After about twenty minutes of paddling, you notice a huge thunderhead looming to the west. It towers high into the atmosphere, and bright white popcorn puffs of clouds build as you watch. The bottom of the cloud is almost black and is already pouring rain. White-pink lightning flashes, and the thunder booms a few seconds later. The storm you feared is a reality! Should you head back to the island?

If you tell Mak and Andrea that you think you should turn around, turn to page 11.

If you say nothing and stick it out, because you're only bound to encounter more storms in this climate, turn to page 24.

"It's not real," Andrea says, staring at the beach with a serious expression. "It can't be real." She keeps paddling hard.

As you approach the shore, the clear, green-blue water around you grows cloudy red and murky. Ghostly figures reach up towards the raft from underwater. They tug on your paddles, trying to wrestle them out of your hands.

You hear an explosive *POP!* and you realize a hole blew in your raft. Then another bursts. Then another. The pale gray, ghostly hands reach over the edges of the raft, pulling the raft down with real strength. You panic. Are you close enough to swim to shore?

You struggle to keep your head above the water, but there are too many slimy hands pulling you down. After a minute, you stop struggling. You realize you don't need air to breathe. You don't need to breathe at all! What freedom you feel, down under the water. You feel weightless and carefree. You look around at the seaweed and coral. Small colorful fish dart here and there. It's quite beautiful—how have you been missing out on this underwater world all this time? You think you could probably stay down here forever.

And you will.

The End

24

You keep your mouth shut and keep on paddling. Mak and Andrea are as determined as you. Miraculously, the storm passes right in front of you, leaving only slightly choppy waters in its wake.

After a while, you can no longer see the island. As much as you didn't enjoy being there, you're uneasy without any land in sight and only a rubber raft beneath you.

Hours pass. Your arms ache. Every so often, you all stop paddling and drift, watching the compass to make sure you're going the right way. Night falls, and you take turns sleeping. The next day dawns bright and clear, with no land or ships on the horizon.

"I could really go for a fish taco right now," Mak says around midday.

"Or a bag of potato chips," Andrea mumbles longingly.

That night, you wake up to Mak shouting: an enormous, brightly lit container ship is headed your way. You fumble for the flare guns, and you and Andrea each shoot one into the night air. The pale pink trails of fire light up your faces with an eerie glow. You all shout at the top of your lungs.

The ship is 100 feet high and probably a thousand feet long. It's lit up, but you doubt anyone is awake at this hour. Mak shoots a third flare, but the ship passes you without slowing down.

The next day, you see another ship far behind you, and you fear you've passed right through the shipping lane. Did you miss Hawaii, too? You can't turn around now—you'd never make it against the current.

Turn to page 26.

"Let's check out the shipwreck," you suggest. Mak looks disappointed but follows you and Andrea.

It takes twenty minutes to walk all the way down the beach. Up close, you realize the ship is massive. Though only part of it is intact, you can see it had four masts and multiple decks. You used to build model ships when you were a kid. You think of some of their names—brigs, schooners, clippers—but those were all smaller, and built for speed. This one looks like a galleon, one of the biggest merchant vessels ever built. They sailed all over the world during the 1600s and 1700s! You also remember that Manila galleons, which regularly sailed and traded between the Philippines and Mexico, discovered many small island chains in the Pacific on their journeys. You've read many legends about ships like this that were lost with treasure on board.

Turn to page 29.

26

Days pass. You run out of water, and then food. It rains, and you collect just enough water to get by for a few more days. But then it doesn't rain for many days. Your lips are dry and cracked. You're so sunburned you can hardly move. On the eighth day, after you run out of water, you wake up from a hazy nap to a beautiful sunset and see a huge, timbered ship emerging from a bank of fog. Its paneled hull is beautifully painted and carved in great detail. It has four masts with billowing, cream colored sails. It's a Spanish galleon, you're sure of it. But these majestic ships haven't been on the seas since the 1800s. Are you dreaming? The ship passes right in front of you. You see the sailors on board are all headless but are walking around on deck like nothing is wrong.

You laugh and fall back against the side of the raft and fall asleep. You won't wake up, and you'll never know where your raft washes ashore. Now you're just one of so many souls lost to the curse of Blood Island.

The End

You walk very close to the ship and shudder, feeling a cold draft.

The ship's upper deck is mostly unbroken and extends about 150 feet from end to end. The whole front of the hull rests on a rocky outcropping. The wide boards are dry and faded gray with salt and sun, and the broken pieces remind you of ragged teeth. The rear of the ship suffered most of the damage and is now mostly a pile of jumbled wood. One small mast remains, its shredded canvas pointing to the sky.

You glance at Mak and notice his eyes are fixed on the prow. The bowsprit at the very front of the ship is still intact and points far out over the water. The figurehead below it is carved with a berobed angel and rearing lions. There's another figure on the bowsprit itself. You realize with a chill that it's a real human skeleton, tied tightly to the wood with thick, fraying rope. You notice that the skull is missing a large piece of bone as well as the lower jaw.

You wonder whether exploring further is a good idea. But you can't stop thinking about the possibility of finding a chest full of Mexican silver on board!

Turn to the next page.

30

You spot a thick, knotted rope hanging over the side of the ship. You give it a sharp tug and decide it's secure. You climb up, hand over hand. Andrea follows close behind you, but Mak stays down below. When you pull yourself over the top, you take a few careful steps in each direction, testing your weight on the boards.

"Mak, come on up! It feels sturdy," you say.

"Nah," he says, "I'll stay here. What are you even looking for?" Mak shouts up to you, sounding worried. "This is probably dangerous...I think you guys should come down."

The careful scientist part of your brain agrees with Mak, but another part seems to have hijacked your senses: if this ship was a galleon, it was either carrying payment or merchandise, and that means a fifty-fifty chance of treasure.

Go on to the next page.

"We'll be quick—I just want to look around a bit," you holler back to Mak. You follow Andrea as she crosses the deck and ducks through a dark doorway into one of the cabins below.

It's empty below deck, as though it was ransacked of every crate, rope, or piece of furniture that might have once filled it. *Chances are the treasure's gone too,* you think.

You look at the ship itself—the wooden boards are smooth with age, and the detailed carving around the doorways evokes another era. It is so different from the sterile white metal construction of *Albatross III*. The boards creak beneath your feet, and you hear the wind whistling eerily through the holes in the hull.

"On second thought, I'm not so sure this is safe either," you say, peering at the thick cobwebs in the dark corners. "I mean, this is amazing, but it really could collapse at any moment."

"Oh I don't know, it seems sturdy to me," Andrea says, slapping the door frame. "Let's go a little farther." She gives you a sly smile.

Turn to the next page.

32

You pass through a low doorway into another empty room. Suddenly you have a splitting pain in your head, a ringing in your ears, and everything in front of you vibrates and blurs. You blink to clear your vision, and notice the room feels warmer. The wood is burnished and new looking. You glance to your right: a candle burns on an ornate desk covered with long rolls of ivory paper, and a man with long curly hair and a dark green suit is sitting at the desk with a quill in his hand. He looks up at you and tries to speak. Blood seeps through his fine, white shirt, dripping down from the ear-to-ear slit across his throat. You gasp and step back as his head thunks down onto the floor and rolls to your feet. His brown eyes are wide open looking at a blood-smeared silver rapier.

You shout and stumble back into the room Andrea is in.

"You're white as a sheet—what happened?"

But you can't speak, only shake your head and point. Andrea walks past you and into the room, and you look over her shoulder, but it's empty.

Turn to page 34.

"Wow! Look at this!" Andrea bends down and picks up the beautiful silver sword, covered in rust instead of blood.

"I saw—" you begin. "I saw—a head, the sword—there was blood...."

Andrea looks at you in alarm.

"Are you feeling okay?" she asks.

"I guess so," you say, sounding anything but.

Andrea continues through another doorway. You don't want to be left alone.

"You coming?" she asks.

If you follow Andrea, turn to page 36.

If you're feeling too uneasy and tell Andrea you are going to head back up on deck instead, turn to page 39.

"Hey, wait," you call out, following Jimmy back onto the beach. He's just a little too far ahead of you.

But Jimmy doesn't slow down. He keeps turning around and smiling at you as he walks, urging you on. You're walking so fast you're almost jogging, while Jimmy keeps a calm, cool pace. And still you can't catch up.

You're almost back to the wreckage of *Albatross III* when Jimmy turns to look at you one last time.

"Good luck, mate!" he chirps, and pulls his head off again, just a little bit, as if he's tipping his hat to you. Then he smiles and turns away. Before you can answer, he vanishes. You stop walking, frustrated that you walked all this way just to have him disappear without any explanation.

You put your hands on your knees and look back at the old shipwrecked galleon. You should probably head back and find Andrea and Mak. But then you hear a noise—a muted, rhythmic thwop-thwop-thwop that gets louder and louder. It takes you a few seconds to recognize the sound of the helicopter rotor. You look up just as the sand around you begins to drift and billow in the wind from the huge spinning blades. The familiar orange and white of the U.S. Coast Guard hovers above you, and you see a pilot peek out the window and wave with a gloved hand. You wave back and suppose you shouldn't be mad at Jimmy Parsons after all.

The End

36

You follow Andrea down six or seven stairs into a long, cavernous space that smells like sea salt.

She takes careful, creaking steps and holds the rusted sword out to one side. You follow and notice shapes leering in the darkness ahead of you in the few glints of light that have filtered all the way down here. As you get close, you realize they are human skeletons, their wrists and ankles bound to the sides of the ship in rusted iron shackles.

"Oh no, Andrea, look…" you say, stopping in your tracks, but she doesn't stop or even turn around. You try again: "I don't like this—I'm going back up."

"Just a little farther," she says. "Don't you want to find the treasure?"

Had you said anything about treasure to her? You keep going, not wanting to be left alone. Without warning, Andrea whirls around pushes you up against the slimy wall, pressing the sword to your throat.

Turn to page 38.

"There's no escaping now," Andrea says in a cold voice you don't recognize. "You dared to disturb our island, and now you will never leave. You will never tell anyone about the things you saw here."

"An—Andrea?!" you stutter. "What are you talking about? What are you doing? It's me!"

"Andrea? Is that the name of the foolish woman who stumbled into the jungle all by herself last night?" The face before you has suddenly transformed—it's not Andrea at all, but a young man with long black hair and a huge scar across his face. "You shouldn't have come here. That man you saw, with his head cut off? He made the same mistake as you did many years ago. I took care of all of them. Sadly, this old blade isn't sharp enough to cut off your head, but I've got another idea."

The man with the scar snaps a set of iron shackles around your wrists and steps back, sneering at you. You tug hard, but the chains are thick and heavy. He laughs at you—a dry, cruel laugh. Then without another word, he turns and walks away. You hear footsteps above you, and you wonder if it's him or if it might be Mak coming to rescue you. But minutes pass and no one comes. You shout Mak's name, even Andrea's name, over and over and over until your throat burns to even breathe. You are alone.

In time your bones will also adorn the inside of this ship, gleaming white in whatever sunlight might ever reach your remains.

The End

"Andrea, I'm heading back," you announce.

You pull yourself back up onto the top deck and look over the edge for Mak, but you don't see him. Perhaps he walked around to the other side. You turn and jump—a person is sitting beside you on the deck, leaning against the gunwale. It's a boy, perhaps twelve or thirteen. He's wearing an old fashioned sailor's outfit, with a cap and a kerchief around his neck. He's working to untie a tangled knot of rope and looks up at you with tired eyes. His face is so pale you feel like you can almost see right through it. You're not sure what to say, but he speaks up first.

"Be careful, eh?" he says casually. "I'd get outta here quick if I was you." His accent is distinctly British.

"Who are you? Where did you come from?" you ask. The hair on your neck is standing up again.

"Name's Jim. Jimmy Parsons. I never made it home. I hope you will—you look like a nice person."

"Where—where's your home?"

"London," says Jimmy, smiling a little bit.

"Well… we're heading to America—California—but you can hitch a ride with us that far…" He's so friendly, you find yourself wanting to help, even though you have no idea if you'll ever make it back home yourself.

Turn to the next page.

40

"It's too late for me," he says resignedly, putting down his rope. He takes off his cap, grabs his thick, dirty blonde hair, and pulls his head clean off. "You see," he says, his mouth moving and his eyebrows bouncing even though there's eight inches of air between the bloody stump of his neck and his head, "I didn't make it off the island alive."

You feel breathless and numb.

"Was this your ship?" you ask, desperate for any information. "What happened to you? How—what—I don't understand—who are you?"

Jimmy puts his head back on and stands up. "Come on, follow me," he says, and walks away from you down the deck toward the rope ladder. But before he reaches it, he disappears. A moment later, he's down on the beach, walking slowly back toward your camp. He looks over his shoulder at you and waves his hand for you to follow him.

If you decide to follow Jimmy, turn to page 35.

If you think things are getting too weird and decide to wait here for your friends, go on to the next page.

You watch Jimmy go, glad to have distance between you and anything that can pull its own head off. *Where on earth are Mak and Andrea?* you think, exasperated.

You look over the side of the ship again. "Mak?" you say cautiously. Maybe he already walked back to camp. Your eyes fall on Jimmy Parsons again, still trotting down the beach by himself, and you take a step backwards to get a better view, not paying attention to where you're going. You bump into an old cannon behind you and fall backwards, smacking the back of your head on the gunwale.

You wake up with no idea what happened and no concept of how long you were out. The light in the sky looks like afternoon. You feel sunburned and sore.

You try to sit up but are stopped by a searing pain in your head. Then the deck starts shaking beneath you. You're sure the old, beat-up ship is about to collapse, but you realize the whole island is shaking.

The mountain erupts with the sound of a thousand dynamite explosions. A gray-black cloud of ash blows high, and massive pieces of rock are hurled through the air in arcs, leaving trails of dust and steam like a jet's contrail. It's followed by a wall of hot gas, mud, and rock hurtling down the mountainside towards you at 400 miles per hour. At that rate, you don't have much time to contemplate your last moments on Earth. But you do say a quick apology in your head to Jimmy Parsons. You might see him sooner than you'd hoped.

The End

42

You mold a bed in the sand, and the sound of the waves lulls you into a deep sleep.

Some time later, you wake up suddenly, your heart racing, with a loud sound echoing in your ears. Was it an explosion? A shout? Maybe it was just a dream.

You feel shivery and hot, like you do when you have a fever, and you suddenly need fresh air. Mak is snoring beside you, and Andrea is still gone.

You grab the flashlight and stumble out onto the beach. You gasp at the beauty of the stars, scattered thick and bright across the blue-black void. It's as if you're on the very edge of the earth, peering right into outer space. You feel so small in the face of the universe and so removed from the life you had a week ago—is this even real? You're suddenly homesick.

A big wave crashes at your feet and startles you out of your daze. As bright as the stars are, there is no moon out, and you can barely see what's in front of you. You can see the dark outline of trees against the sky, and you can tell where the gray beach ends and the black jungle begins.

A scream cuts through the night, shrill and close by. You think it might have been a woman's voice but can't be sure. Was it Andrea?

Go on to the next page.

Mak is still asleep in the lean-to.

You get the prickly feeling again, like someone is behind you. You spin around.

A figure is standing on the beach, about a hundred yards away. You can barely see as it is, but it's clearly the shape of a person.

"Andrea!" you say, just loud enough for her to hear. You wave, but the figure doesn't move or answer. Icy fear slips into your stomach.

Turn to the next page.

44

You have a flashlight in your hand, but you're afraid to turn it on. You hold your breath.

And then it's closer. Did it move? It's only fifty yards away now, and you feel it looking right at you. Then suddenly it's only ten yards away. You can't tell if it's a man or a woman—its clothes are baggy and shapeless, its hair long and matted, and its face is filthy and oddly shaped.

You point the flashlight ahead of you and click it on.

Turn to page 46.

46

The flashlight bulb explodes in a burst of white light. You blink hard and drop it in the sand. At the same time, the thing in front of you emits a ghastly shriek. You fall to your knees in the darkness and don't dare look up.

LEAVE THIS PLACE! you hear inside your head, in a gravelly voice that's not your own. It's as if the words were fed directly into your brain from the creature. You think, *who are you?* and you get a raspy reply almost instantly.

I am the guardian of the island. I hold the spirits of everyone who died here. I am everyone who came and never left. I could be you if you're not careful.

How did you become the guardian? you ask.

I was beheaded by a terrible ruler. I was thrown into a volcano as a human sacrifice. I was starved in a prison cell for a crime I did not commit. I caught the plague and my feet and hands rotted off, and no one knew how to save me. Sometimes, my heart was cut out of my body and eaten while I was still alive. I was buried and burned when the mountain erupted.

What can I do? you think.

LEAVE! Leave the island, it says again.

But... I can't, you think. *There's no way off, our ship is ruined...*

If you don't leave soon, you never will, it says.

Go on to the next page.

You don't move. You're just barely formulating this thought: *How do I get off the island?* when it answers you:

Trust me.

Trust you? How? you think.

If you want your life back, you must look death in the eye. It extends one rotten-looking hand and beckons for you to approach it.

If you trust it and choose to "face death,"
turn to page 48.

If you decide to wake up Mak, turn to page 50.

You force yourself to put one foot in front of the other and walk slowly toward the creature.

As you get close, its appearance doesn't get any clearer. It's human-like but definitely something other than just human. It's blurry around the edges, and you feel like you can't focus anywhere except on its own eyes—glittering and black, as shiny and depthless as an insect's.

When you're close enough, you can see your own reflection in its eyes. You look small and weak, standing here alone on the beach. Then you see yourself lying on the beach, sunburned and starving. You see yourself drowning in shallow water. You see yourself running through the jungle, being chased by something. You see the volcano erupting and burying the entire island.

These are only some of the possibilities, says the figure. *Death will come to all of us one day, but we don't know how it will happen. While you have looked into my eyes, I have looked into yours. I have seen what you have done so far in your life and what you still wish to do before you die. You have a good heart and noble aspirations—don't let go of them. And don't forget: no matter where you are, no matter who you are, death will come to you again one day. And you won't know when.*

Go on to the next page.

As you struggle to understand, you realize the figure is fading. As the dark silhouette dissolves into the night air, you look right through where its body once was. Your eyes land on the bright lights of a passing ship!

"Help!" you scream. You run to the emergency pack and grab two flare guns, shooting them into the sky above your head. The fiery pink trails sear across the night sky. You wait under the dying light as the ship begins to turn around. Death just gave you a second chance at life. You're not going to waste it.

The End

50

You turn around and whisper into the lean-to: "Mak! Wake up! Come here!" Mak doesn't wake up, and when you turn around, the thing is gone. You scramble back to the lean-to wondering if you've just had a bout of sleepwalking. The next thing you know it's morning.

Andrea returned in the night, sometime after you fell asleep, with a bucket full of water.

"What happened last night? Are you okay?" you ask her in the comforting light of morning.

"It was awful," she says. "I got lost and heard screaming. I don't know what it was, probably some kind of monkey. It's a miracle I found my way back." You feel guilty for not going with her.

All three of you are jumpy and paranoid, and hungry. You search all day but find no other source of food on the island. Not one wild fruit, not one animal, not one fish or crab or snail in the water. It's like the island itself is lacking a life source.

After a few more days, your energy bars run out. Thanks to Andrea, you have a source of fresh water, but you've got to find more food.

Days pass and no one comes to rescue you. You fiddle with the radios and send SOS messages into the sky. Sometimes you see airline jets high overhead and think about writing "HELP" in the sand, though you know they're way too high up to see it.

Go on to the next page.

One night, you hear a noise that wakes you up. Andrea and Mak are awake too. All three of you walk out of the lean-to and see the figure standing on the beach. It's almost comforting, like you're seeing an old friend. You, Mak, and Andrea walk forward and join it in the darkness.

The End

"Sorry Mak, I'm with Andrea on this one," you say. "And I don't think anyone should go in there alone."

"Okay," he says with some dismay. "I'll stay here and figure something out." He looks at the wrecked ship. "Good luck," he adds.

You and Andrea each grab a bucket from the pile of wreckage and head toward the jungle. The sun is almost at the horizon. Andrea steps into the shade, through a slight break in the vines, and you follow right behind her.

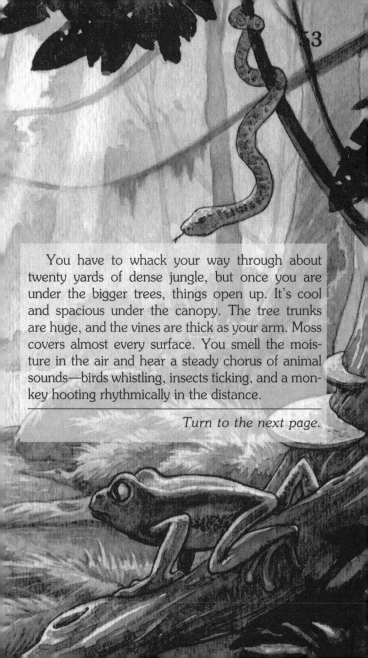

You have to whack your way through about twenty yards of dense jungle, but once you are under the bigger trees, things open up. It's cool and spacious under the canopy. The tree trunks are huge, and the vines are thick as your arm. Moss covers almost every surface. You smell the moisture in the air and hear a steady chorus of animal sounds—birds whistling, insects ticking, and a monkey hooting rhythmically in the distance.

Turn to the next page.

54

"I can hear water!" you say as soon as you pick out the familiar trickling gurgle from the other sounds.

"You're right!" Andrea says, slowing down and cocking her head. "Where is it?"

You've been following a faint path—it's narrow, but there is a visible trail on the spongy forest floor, where someone or something has walked many times before. "What do you think uses this path?" you ask in a low voice.

"Oh, anything. Maybe the monkeys," Andrea says, sounding distracted, as if it didn't matter. You think it matters very much.

You look behind you, thinking you hear a stick snapping, and when you turn back, you see you've reached a fork.

"Hmm," Andrea says, squinting into the trees. "What do you think? Right or left? Or maybe we should split up and double our chances of success."

"Or failure," you say. The right path seems to head straight into an especially dense thicket of trees, and the left curves away up a slight hill. You don't see any obvious advantage to either option.

If you decide to split up, go on to page 55.

If you decide to take the right path together, turn to page 64.

If you decide to take the left path together, turn to page 72.

"Maybe we should split up," you say, looking between the two paths helplessly. "It's going to be dark soon, and we don't want to waste any more time."

"Okay," Andrea takes a deep breath. "Just...be careful. Don't go off the path."

You nod and give her a small smile. Then you turn and set off down the right path, into the dense jungle.

"Let's meet back here in five minutes!" she calls after you.

"Okay!" you shout over your shoulder.

As soon as Andrea is out of sight, you regret your decision to split up. One by one, the birds stop their cheerful noises. You hear your own heavy breathing. A breeze picks up, and you hear a rustling. You aren't sure if it's the wind or something more sinister.

You can't hear the trickling water anymore. Did you take a wrong turn somewhere and veer off the path? You decide to just go back to the fork and wait for Andrea. You definitely hear the snap of a stick at your back, and you whirl around. Nothing is there. You feel a surge of adrenaline—your heart pounds and it's hard to breathe. Your neck prickles, and you whirl around again. Nothing is there. You realize you're gripping the handle of the bucket so tightly it's cutting your palm.

Turn to the next page.

56

You start retracing your path, stepping slowly and carefully.

You feel a drop of water fall on your face. *Rain!* you think, but as you rub the raindrop from your cheek, it feels wrong. You look down and your hand is streaked with blood. Horrified, you look up into the tree above you, but nothing is there.

You run. Roots catch your water-logged shoes, and vines whip your face. You are sure you hear something behind you, but you dare not look back. Suddenly the path disappears. You skid to a halt and turn around to find where you veered off of it, but all you see are trees and vines and ground cover in a uniform circle around you. No path at all.

"Andrea!" you shout. You know you're lost. "Andreaaa!" Your throat burns from yelling so loudly.

You swallow hard, fighting your fear.

Turn to page 59.

"Wh-what do you want?" you stutter. "Who are you?"

The man hasn't moved—he's just standing there, no more than ten feet away. You force yourself to look back up at his face.

"Glen?!" you shout, in horror. Glen was your classmate at the university—he was on the ship with you! You peer at his bloody face, still half-hidden in shadow. Could it really be him? Then you hear his unmistakable voice in your head, as if he's speaking right into your brain:

Don't be afraid. Don't run.

"Are you—are you okay?" you ask aloud, aware of how stupid that sounds.

I'm not, but it doesn't matter now, his voice says. *I didn't make it through the shipwreck alive. You, Mak, and Andrea were the only ones.*

Your heart falls at these words.

Listen, he says, *this island does have a curse. The rumors are all true. You're smart—I always thought you were—so use your head. Don't do anything stupid. You have to make it off this island alive.*

"But how?" you ask hopelessly. "I'm lost—I don't even know how to find my way back to the beach!"

Glen's ghost steps sideways and points. A hundred yards away, you see Andrea standing, hands on her hips, looking around her. *She's waiting for you,* he says.

Turn to page 62.

Something moves through the trees in front of you. You stand as still as a statue, until you can see it clearly: a man in a bloodstained T-shirt stands fifty feet away. He has a metal bar protruding from one ruined eye socket and out the back of his head. His face is covered in dark blood.

Your own head spins and your breath is shallow. This can't be real, you think, with a wave of nausea.

"Andreaaa!" you yell again. The man vanishes in front of you. Then you feel something at your back, the heat of something almost touching you. You turn and see the man, right behind you, glistening with blood. There is something familiar about him, but the stake though his eye is so horrible you can hardly look. You're frozen with fear, but maybe he's not going to hurt you. Then again, if he wanted to help you, why is he still just standing there like a zombie?

If you speak up and ask the zombie man what he wants, turn to page 57.

If you take the offensive and hit him with your bucket, turn to page 60.

60

You clench the bucket handle in both fists and swing it as hard as you can in a wide arc, smacking him hard right in the face. He steps backwards a bit in surprise but doesn't fall over. He must have superhuman strength—you hadn't counted on that.

You throw the bucket in his face and turn and run as hard as you've ever run before. Your panic has taken over completely and you pay no attention to where you're going. You're sure that at any moment you'll feel his iron grip on your shoulder. But instead you find yourself tumbling head over heels down a steep embankment. You land hard on your back, and the wind is knocked out of you.

You try to sit up and notice your right leg won't move. Actually, it hurts. It really, really hurts. You prop yourself up on your elbows just as a thick, black snake coils around your leg.

Go on to the next page.

The enormous snake has patterned scales on its back, gleaming blood red in the twilight. You see a blood-dark bite mark at your ankle. You can no longer feel your foot, your leg feels like it's on fire, and the heat is creeping up into your thigh, now into your abdomen.

The venom is spreading. You grit your teeth.

The slithering thing advances, now inches away from your face, and flicks its forked tongue, tasting your fear. Delirious, you flick your tongue back at it. Its cloudy eyes blink once, slowly, and then you feel the white hot sting of fangs sunk into the tender flesh of your neck. But only for a second.

The End

Be careful, Glenn says forcefully, and then he steps backwards into the shadows and disappears. You take off through the underbrush toward Andrea.

"Andrea!" you call out as you get nearer.

"There you are!" she says, exasperated. "That was way more than five minutes. Any luck?"

"Not really—you?" you say.

"Me neither. I turned back almost right away. I was too afraid of getting lost on my own."

Should you tell her about Glen? You still can't believe what just happened, and while you're dying to say something, she might think you're crazy. Maybe you should just look for water on the other path, as far away from Glen's ghost as you can get.

*If you tell her about Glen's ghost,
go on to page 63.*

*If you keep your mouth shut and stay away
from that part of the island, turn to page 72.*

"Holy Toledo!" Andrea gasps, after you finish your story about losing the path and Glen's ghost.

"He said to be careful, so I think we should stick together from now on," you say.

"I agree," Andrea says with a serious look. "My path didn't look promising—did you get very far down that one?"

"No," you admit. "I veered off it pretty quickly, so maybe we should try it again."

Andrea nods but looks a little bit worried.

Turn to the next page.

64

"Water is going to run downhill," you say, "so going right really is our best bet."

"Okay, good point," Andrea agrees, and you set off down the right-hand path.

You part a stand of giant ferns and sweep vines away from your feet. The sound of trickling water remains steady. As you continue, the path becomes clearer and wider. Suddenly you both stop short, staring at the imposing structure in front of you.

It's very tall and very wide, built of large blocks of gray-brown stone. It's pointed, like a pyramid, but the intricacy of the carvings in the stone and the wide entrance reminds you more of a shrine or a temple. You still hear water trickling but don't see it anywhere.

You and Andrea approach the entrance. The stone is blotched with moss and lichen and strangled in thick vines, but beneath the growth you see exquisite carvings of animal shapes and faces. You enter the thick stone doorway into a cavernous room. The ceiling is open to the sky, letting in a little bit of light. The stone floor has symbols and lines cut into it, making geometric patterns that look intentional and mathematic. The room surrounds a shallow pool, no more than a foot or two deep, fed by a channel of water.

Andrea gasps, looking up at the walls around you. Your eyes have adjusted to the low light, and you realize what she sees: the walls, which go up about three stories, are piled with human bones. You're in a tomb.

Turn to page 66.

66

"I've heard of these places," Andrea says very quietly, "—ossuaries, charnel houses—mostly in Europe or on small islands, where they don't have a lot of land available to bury people. Every few years, they dig up the bones and store them somewhere, to make room for new bodies in the cemeteries."

There is a shelf about halfway up the wall where skulls are lined up neatly, all facing you. You feel like all of the dark, empty eye sockets are watching you.

"Maybe we should go—this doesn't feel right," you say.

"I agree. But let's grab some water quickly." Andrea picks up her bucket and walks toward the pool in the center. "Think it's clean?" she asks, kneeling down in front of it. You join her. The water is crystal clear. Almost too clear. It has an odd silvery shine. Maybe it's from the stone at the bottom of the pool? As you stare at the water, you see shapes rippling in and out: people's faces, hands, open mouths and wide eyes. You can also feel their emotions—desperation, pain, and fear.

"Hang on," you say. "Are you sure it's safe?"

"Well, I agree this place is unpleasant, but…yeah, I think it's fine," she says. "It's just water, right?"

Go on to the next page.

Maybe you're overreacting. You are very dehydrated. You look back into the pool: the water is clear and empty. Maybe you imagined it after all. You could let Andrea drink it first just to be safe.

If you cast aside your doubt and relieve your thirst, turn to page 68.

If you let Andrea drink it first, turn to page 69.

"You're right," you say, shaking your head. "It's probably fine."

You lean down and lift a handful of cool water from the pool to your parched lips. It's the sweetest, clearest, most delicious water you've ever tasted in your life. You sigh with relief and—without warning, your insides are on fire. You look into the pool and see the faces again. They all rise to the surface, and their mouths are wide open, shrieking in rage. You feel their pain echoing inside you.

It turns out you've consumed a human soul from the Pool of Eternity, for which there is no cure. Only one soul can live in a body at once, and when two are present, the energy is too great, and they destroy each other.

Your bones will also stay forever in this ancient tomb, though they won't be stacked nicely around the walls. At least not for awhile.

The End

"Okay, well, you first," you say.

Andrea looks at you in surprise, then looks back at the pool. She takes a deep breath and reaches toward the water with cupped hands when a deafening clatter causes you both to jump. A skull and a bone have just toppled off their places in the wall and rolled to a rattling halt on the stone floor right next to you.

The skull is lying on its side, and its wide mouth and huge eye sockets gape at you in a silent, mirthless laugh.

"Whoa," Andrea whispers, and sits back on her heels, gazing at the skull. "What are the chances of that happening? These bones haven't moved in hundreds of years." You realize you're in a cold sweat, and you stand up to leave, but Andrea is fixated on the water.

Turn to page 71.

"Andrea, hey!" She's leaning farther and farther down toward the water. You grab her by the elbow and yank her to her feet. "Andrea! What are you doing?"

She looks at you and blinks rapidly, shaking her head. "Sorry," she says, looking confused and embarrassed. "Sorry—don't know what came over me." She glances back at the sideways skull and her eyes linger on it.

Almost before you realize what you're doing, you grab Andrea's hand tightly and kick the skull right into the pool. As soon as it touches the water, a wind-torn shrieking sound fills the room. The skull, now at the bottom of the shallow pool, turns black and then explodes into a ball of smoking fire, evaporating the water with a burst of hissing steam.

You both shout in surprise and run out of the building as fast as you can. Without stopping, you both run all the way back to the fork in the path.

The air is lighter. The birds are singing once again. The evil feeling from the ossuary is gone.

"On second thought, I guess that water wasn't good to drink," Andrea says. "What now?"

Turn to the next page.

72

You point up the hill to the left. "Let's head up there together. We'll have a better view of things, including any water sources," you say.

"All right," Andrea says. "Lead the way."

You climb and climb, following the trail, but you never reach a spot with a view. The trickling water sound fades in and out, and you wonder at times if you're imagining it.

Eventually the trees open up and you reach a clearing at the base of the mountain. It is steeper and more magnificent up close. Your eye is drawn to the dark, yawning mouth of a large cave. You and Andrea approach it in silence. When you stand in the entrance, you guess the ceiling must be forty or fifty feet above you, like the vaulted ceilings of a Gothic cathedral, and it continues deep into the earth for hundreds of yards before disappearing into darkness. The walls are made of a rough, ivory stone, streaked with rust-red horizontal lines.

Go on to the next page.

"Wow, look at this…" Andrea says in a low voice. She examines the wall of the cave. You realize the rust-red markings covering the cave walls are actually paintings. You see images of the mountain and of animals—birds, fish, some sort of four-legged creature. There are clear representations of water and even of human beings, of houses, of plants, trees, ships. Men with helmets? And swords? It's really hard to make out in the darkness, and they continue on deep into the cave where no light shines.

"This is incredible," Andrea says. "We have to come back here tomorrow when there's more light."

"Shh!" you say suddenly. "I hear water!" The sound of rushing water is coming from deep inside the cave. You walk a little farther in and find a stream of fresh water cutting a path through the stone floor of the cave—an underground spring. You fill your buckets.

"We'll come back tomorrow with Mak," Andrea says.

When you return to the beach, you see that Mak has constructed a rough little lean-to from the wreckage. He has also built a small fire and is sitting in front of it eating another energy bar.

Turn to the next page.

74

"I was starting to worry about you two!" he exclaims in relief, standing up.

Andrea hoists her bucket. "We come bearing water!" she says triumphantly. "And you just have to come back with us tomorrow to see what else we found."

You ease down in front of the fire and try to relax as Andrea tells Mak all about the cave paintings. You're no longer hungry or thirsty, and you're suddenly exhausted. You think about home and feel a twinge of sadness—you wonder if anyone knows about your shipwreck. Surely a rescue crew must be looking for you already. The island is big enough to be seen from the air, and you can't be that far from Hawaii.

At least you have the protection of the lean-to tonight while you sleep.

Turn to page 76.

"Take a look at this …" Andrea pokes at something on the ground with a stick. You catch up with her on the trail. She's examining a pile of brown shiny pellets, each the size of a chicken egg.

You lean close then back away a little bit when you realize what you're looking at. "Oh, wow, is that…?"

"Bird excrement," she says. "And it's very large, which means it belongs to a very large bird. Larger than I expected…" She sounds excited but a little nervous. "You can see here…these are seeds…it's been eating some sort of fruit…"

Mak is hanging back and looking impatient and anxious. "You guys, I think we should head back. What if someone's sent a rescue team to get us, but we're not on the beach when they arrive?"

Andrea sighs. "I'd really like to keep going. I came here for this bird, and if it exists, I want proof." She sounds like she means it and looks at you with her eyebrows raised. "Don't you?"

You think you feel the ground rumble again, but before you can say anything, you hear another crashing sound in the trees farther uphill.

If you decide to go with Andrea to look for the crested adzebill, turn to page 80.

If you think it's best to stick with your goal of finding help and getting rescued, turn to page 89.

76

"Wow!" Mak says, staring up at the cave walls the next morning. "These are amazing!"

Andrea is pacing back and forth, hands on her hips, squinting up at the higher paintings. "Boy, I wish I had my glasses," she says breathlessly. "Just incredible."

It's early morning, and there is enough light to see more paintings than you could the night before.

"My gosh," says Mak, "look." He points to a painting of a beach lined with tall stakes. Stuck on each stake is a human head with red blood pooled underneath. The image makes you uneasy.

"I hope whoever made that painting was drawing from their imagination and not reality," you say quietly.

You stare for a moment at a small scene depicting two figures: a person and another large creature. A dinosaur? Can't be. A bird? A really big bird. Wait, this looks like the crested adzebill! You notice its wide triangular beak, thick legs, and the horn-like casque atop its head, like the Australian cassowary.

Andrea wanders over to look with you.

"Oh my..." she says.

"Could this be...the adzebill?" you say.

"I have a good feeling about this!" she says with a smile.

Turn to page 78.

"So, you guys," Mak pipes up from behind you. "This is really cool and all, but we still need to focus on getting off this island." He's looking at you help-lessly. "What if we're stuck here forever?" he says in a quieter voice. It looks like he's really worried.

Andrea sighs but doesn't say anything.

"Mak," you say, "we're going to be fine. We have each other, and we have supplies from the ship." You try to smile, but he reminds you that adzebill aside, you are still shipwrecked. "I have an idea," you continue. "Why don't we try to climb this mountain? We'll be able to see the whole island—there must be something useful to us that we couldn't see from the beach."

It takes the three of you about an hour to climb a steep few hundred feet of the mountainside. The sun is still obscured by thick, dark clouds, but the temperature and humidity keep rising as the hours pass. You're drenched in sweat, and you're followed by a cloud of tiny, obnoxious flies. The terrain is becoming more shrubby and rocky the higher you go.

You skid on some loose gravel and skin your knee. Your legs are getting tired. You feel an odd vertigo, like your body is too heavy while your head feels light and tippy.

"Whew!" Andrea pauses and exhales. "Wel-come to the tropics!"

Mak grunts and wipes some flies off the back of his neck.

Go on to the next page.

You reach a clearing in the trees where you can see the mountain rolling away beneath you and the tops of trees like little rounded broccoli crowns. You still don't have a vantage point of the other side of the island. You all agree to keep going up the mountain a little farther. As you take that next step, you experience the vertigo again. It's like there's a magnetic field making the air thick and heavy and hard to move through. The ground trembles slightly but distinctly, and you hear a very deep, very faint rumble, like far away thunder. Then it stops, and your vertigo is gone.

"Whoa, did you guys feel that?" you ask.

"Feel what?" Andrea says turning around in concern.

"Uh, yeah," Mak says, looking around, and then asks, "Is this a volcano? Did you make me climb a volcano?"

"What? What did you feel?" Andrea asks looking around.

Just then you hear a crashing sound in the brush up ahead.

You're all silent for a moment before Mak says, "Great, something else that's about to kill me."

"Oh Mak, don't be so dramatic!" Andrea says and starts uphill ahead of you.

Turn to page 75.

80

"Okay, Andrea, but let's be quick about it," you say. "I want to find the adzebill as much you do, but it's not worth getting lost."

Mak sighs in resignation but follows along. You continue hearing sticks snapping and seeing rustling up ahead. You check behind you to make sure you're not getting too far off the path. When you turn back around, you almost walk right into Andrea because she's stopped at the foot of a giant boulder. On top of the boulder is the largest bird's nest you've ever seen.

What surprises you more than its massive size are the baby birds in the nest, each about the size of a full-grown chicken. Under different circumstances, you would find their appearance almost funny—they're mostly featherless, with bright pink wrinkly skin, giant pop-eyes, and hooked beaks. Their tiny, pointy wings have a few wispy, white feathers poking out, and they flap around helplessly in excitement while making a sort of hiccuping, cheeping sound.

Go on to the next page.

You figure you've probably scared the chicks, but you hear another rustling sound behind you, and you to turn to see a bird twice as tall as Mak emerging from the shrubbery. You know immediately that this is an unknown species. It could even be some unnatural mutation, you think. Or something prehistoric left undisturbed on the island for millions of years. It looks just like you expected the crested adzebill to look, except ten times bigger.

Turn to the next page.

The bird glares down at you. You are intruders in its home. The blue-green feathers down her back are iridescent, while the rest of her is a mottled, warm russet brown. Her feet are the size of truck tires lying flat, each one with claws the size of your forearm. Her bright yellow eyes flicker with intelligence as she evaluates the three of you, and the crest on her head, bright red and the size of a serving platter, is everything you'd hoped for and more. Her bill is very wide and thick, and probably strong enough to rip your arm off.

"Holy…." Mak trails off. He's as pale as a ghost.

Andrea's expression mirrors yours—eyes bright with wonder.

"What should we do?" you whisper, looking the adzebill in the eye. You guess she's trying to figure out if you're a threat or food. Or both.

"Don't move," Andrea says firmly. "Don't run. If you run, she'll think you're prey, and then she'll catch up and kill you." Mak doesn't look convinced. "Don't. Move." Andrea repeats.

If you decide to run, turn to page 84.

*If you decide to stand your ground,
turn to page 86.*

84

You trust Andrea's knowledge, but this is different—no one's ever studied this bird. Plus, your life depends on it.

"I can't," you whisper. "I'm outta here—Mak, you coming? On three? One… two…"

"No!" Andrea says.

You and Mak sprint in the opposite direction. Your fear propels you, and you're surprised at how fast you're moving. You wonder if Andrea is following you, so you venture a look back—but all you see is the adzebill, charging towards you like a freight train, with her enormous powerful beak trained on your head.

It's a shame the world will never know she exists, but tonight the baby adzebills will have the best meal of their lives. At least you contribute in this small way to the survival of such a magnificent species.

The End

"I think Andrea's right, Mak—don't move," you say. You look at the adzebill and think, *Don't be afraid, I'm not your enemy.* You reach into your pocket for an energy bar. The great, beautiful bird cocks her head suddenly at the movement of your arm.

"What are you doing?" Mak whispers urgently. "You just said not to move!"

"Trust me," you say. "If she wants to eat us, she'll eat us whether we run or not." You unwrap the energy bar very slowly and hold it out at arm's length.

The adzebill cocks her head the other way, eying your hand very carefully. Then she runs at you full speed. You squeeze your eyes shut, but she stops short, just a foot in front of you. She's leaning down, looking into your eyes. You're breath is coming in shaky waves. *Please let this work*, you think.

Then the adzebill slowly, tenderly, carefully plucks the energy bar out of your open palm and swallows it whole. She stands up tall again, takes a few enormous steps around you, and settles down in her nest next to her cheeping chicks. Mak drops to the ground.

Go on to the next page.

Andrea bends down to help Mak up and gives you a grin.

"Nice job," she says. "I admit, I was nervous for a second there, you know, when it charged us like an angry bull."

You grin back. "Me too. This is amazing, isn't it?"

The adzebill hasn't forgotten about you. She glances up every once in awhile from her nest but doesn't look worried. She trusts you now. She's preening herself while the chicks bob around and wait for someone to feed them.

Just then, your two-way radio crackles:

"Can anybody hear me? This is the United States Coast Guard searching for the crew of *Albatross III*. Come in—over."

"Affirmative!" you shout into your radio. "This is the crew of *Albatross III*! Over!"

"Reading you loud and clear. We've got a bird circling you. Can you make it to the beach? Over."

"A bird?!" Mak says in alarm.

You laugh. "Don't worry, that's military talk for helicopter." Then, into the radio, "Roger. See you on the beach."

You take one last look back at the adzebill in her nest and wonder if you'll ever make it back here someday, and if not, whether the world will believe what you've seen. On your way to the beach, you find a two-foot-long feather and tuck it in your belt thinking, *Bird DNA in the hand is worth a family of birds in the bush!*

The End

"I agree this is important," you say to Andrea with a sigh, "but I really don't think we have time for this right now."

She gives you a hard stare. "Fine," she says, her lips tight, and starts to walk down the mountain at a quick clip.

Descending the mountain is easier than climbing up. You reach the clearing in the trees where you admired the view of the sloping mountain before. The sky has turned a bright, cloudless blue and the sun is hot. You smell something spicy. You see wisps of gray smoke trickling out of the trees down below.

Rescue! you think. But then you get a better look and realize there's an entire village below you—thatched roofs, mud homes, cleared fields with dark soil that you could have sworn were just full of trees a few minutes ago. You see people—people!—down there, some working in the fields, some standing near the small houses. Children are running. You hear laughter and you smell cooking meat. You feel a sense of peace.

Turn to the next page.

"Hey you guys!" you shout. The three of you stand and stare.

"That wasn't there before," says Mak.

"...But it had to be," says Andrea.

"How could we not have noticed?" says Mak.

"Come on!" you shout. "Maybe they can help us!" You and Mak start running down the path, with Andrea, seeming hesitant, bringing up the rear.

It must have taken you hours to climb so high, but it seems only minutes until your downward path levels out and you hear human voices weaving through the trees ahead. The sounds pull you through the jungle in desperation.

Go on to the next page.

Mak is ahead of you, but he has stopped behind a large tree at the edge of a clearing, his finger to his lips, warning you to be quiet. Andrea catches up, breathing hard, leaning down with hands on her knees. There is a group of kids, teenagers maybe, working the soil in the cleared field not far away from you. They are laughing and joking together as they drag long poles through the dirt, breaking up the clumps. Mak points out a small structure, a hut with clay walls and a thatched roof, at the edge of the field. It looks like a home. You see a woman with a small child on her hip disappear through the dark doorway.

If you think you're better off approaching the woman in the house, turn to the next page.

If you think you should approach the kids in the field to ask for help, turn to page 95.

Andrea leads the way toward the mud house. She walks slowly and deliberately, and you try to stay calm behind her. She peeks around the door and says something quietly. You and Mak stay outside, but a second later, you hear a bloodcurdling scream, and Andrea jumps back out looking shaken.

"Bad idea," she says, "maybe we should go."

But people are already running toward the hut, and before you can make an escape, you're surrounded by a dozen or so men with glittering weapons. Looks like you're not going anywhere. Without listening to your pleas, a group of tattooed men tie your hands and march you through the village. You stop at the same cave that you and Andrea discovered the day before. Deep inside the cave, you're led down a narrow stairway into a pit filled with prison cells. They put all three of you in the farthest, darkest cell. You're left there without a word.

You wonder if anyone will ever come down to your cell again, or if this is supposed to be your final punishment.

Turn to page 94.

The next morning, you're awoken by the same group of tattooed men. You and Mak and Andrea are led out of the pit along with three other prisoners who, by their dirty clothing and skeletal frames, look like they've been down there a long time. It's a bright sunny day, and the morning air is cool and fresh. The other prisoners are mumbling monotonously, as if in prayer.

You're heading towards the mountain, which has a cap of clouds obscuring the very top.

After a treacherous climb made even more difficult and slow by the fact that your hands are tied, you reach the top of the mountain. It's a volcano! The crater is enormous and deep and filled with a green-blue pool of boiling water. You can feel the steam from here and see the air rippling with waves of heat. All six of you are lined up with swords at your backs.

The handle of the sword pushes you hard, and you fly forward through the steamy air. But just before you hit the water, everything around you dissolves into white mist, like the cloud that covered up the top of the mountain.

You wake up on the beach, tired and wet and sore. The wreckage of *Albatross III* lays out in front of you. Mak emerges, looking dazed. Andrea stands beside you.

It's the shipwreck, you realize. *It's just happened. I've traveled through time!*

Was that all a failure? Or is this another chance at success? To find out, turn back to page 10.

You nod toward the field, and the others agree with you. You step out of the trees and walk slowly, calmly, toward the group of kids in the field. You're out in front with Mak, and Andrea is just behind you. One of the kids sees you and immediately his smile drops, along with his digging tool. The others turn around. You raise your hands up in front of you, showing them you mean no harm. You walk slowly. They just stare at you like they're seeing ghosts.

Suddenly, one of them turns and runs back toward the village, and immediately afterwards the others follow him, throwing down their sticks in the soil. You sigh and turn around to Mak and Andrea.

"I hope we didn't scare them too badly," you say, dismayed. "What should we do?"

"Uh, we may not get to make that decision," says Andrea sternly, squinting at something over your shoulder.

Turn to the next page.

You whirl back around and see a group of a dozen men marching across the field almost as fast as those kids ran. You take a few steps backwards, once again raising your hands in surrender. Before you have a chance to think about running away, you're surrounded.

"Hello," Andrea says tentatively, "Do you... speak English?"

The men are all carrying silver broadswords of different sizes. Their faces and upper bodies are tattooed in intricate, beautiful patterns of blue-black ink, reminding you of Mak's tattoo. At Andrea's greeting, they whisper to each other in a language you don't recognize. Their words spin around you, around the circle they've made. The sun keeps getting in your eyes.

And then they blindfold you. At the same time, someone grabs your hands and binds them tightly behind you. By the sounds of struggling around you, you guess they've done the same to Mak and Andrea.

A sharp point in your back compels you forward. You march.

The men make you walk for a long time. Up hills, down stairways, in sunlight and shade. You trip often, over rocks, down embankments. They don't say anything, but someone always lifts you roughly to your feet again and then points you in the right direction before you start walking again.

Go on to the next page.

Eventually, you feel the air become cool and moist, as if you've entered a cave. You're given one final shove, and then they're gone. You stand still for a few moments, to make sure they're really gone, before you feel your way around. You bump into a rough stone wall and use it to drag the blindfold off your face. You're in a dark, damp cell with a dirt floor. There are no windows. There is a door made of tree trunks tied together, and you can see through the cracks that your cell is one of many in a circle at the bottom of a deep, gloomy pit.

You hear things coming from the other cells, but the noises echo around the circular space making it impossible to know their origin. You hear moaning, tapping, creaking. You hear gibberish jabbering in a high pitched voice. You hear liquid dripping. You hear nervous laughter that makes your hair stand on end. You hear crying, sobbing, wailing. Occasionally, you hear tortured screams.

Turn to the next page.

You have no sense of time here—has one hour passed, or five? You are hungry and sunburned and your head is pounding again. Your arms ache so badly from being tied behind your back. You want to slide down the cell wall and just have all of this disappear. You think of Mak and Andrea—where are they?

You go to your door and say in as calm a voice as you can summon: "Andrea? Are you here? Mak?"

A muffled reply comes:

"Yes! Here! Mak?"

"Where are you?"

"Andrea?"

"What's going on?"

Their voices overlap. They're talking to each other as well as you, which means you're all in separate cells, though you can't tell which ones. The sound of their voices is clear and hopeful over the gruesome sounds elsewhere in the pit, like a sudden radio signal.

Radio signal! You'd nearly forgotten about the two-way radio in your pocket.

You hear footsteps, and you peer through the cracks in the door. Your door flies open and you're faced with two tattooed men holding gold-handled cutlasses that look like they belonged to pirates. They each grab one of your arms and march you up a staircase along one side of the pit. You hear footsteps behind you and manage to glimpse Mak being similarly manhandled, right before you are blindfolded again.

Turn to page 100.

"Andrea," you say quietly, "I'm going to take your radio…" She turns around so you can take it easily from the clip on her belt. Then you say to them both, "The door is open—let's make a run for it when I say…"

You hold both radios behind your back and turn the volume all the way up.

"NOW!" you shout, and at the same time you hold the radios in front of you, facing each other, and hold down the transmit buttons to create a feedback loop. The resulting sound is even louder than you expected—piercing, squealing, and grating, like a bow being violently dragged across an untuned violin. The king and the guards all cover their ears and cower in fear at the sound. All three of you dash for the door, but the king reacts quicker than you think—he's shouting after you, and when you're halfway down the narrow, curling stairway, you're blocked by a mob of guards with swords. There is no way out.

You are marched back up to the king's room, where he is waiting with the small silver knife in his hand. He speaks to you in a soft, dangerous voice, and Mak translates:

"I do not doubt you have magic. You proved that well. But clearly you want to use your powers against me, which I cannot allow. I am going to cut out your hearts and eat them, and then I will have your power for myself. If you truly are immortals like you say, you will not need your mortal heart to survive."

The king looks right at you, holding the knife up a little higher, and says one more thing: "You first."

The End

100

When your blindfold is removed, you're surprised to see that you're in a beautiful room with smooth stone walls and silver ornaments—mirrors, knives, necklaces, and bowls shine from every surface. A window looks down onto a beach. You are high on a hill. You wonder if this room belongs to someone important. Then you turn around and see that someone.

From his thick silver crown, you know right away he's royalty. He doesn't have tattoos like the men who brought you here and stand behind him like bodyguards. His hair is very long and hangs below his shoulders. But the most notable thing about his appearance is an enormous scar that runs from his right eyebrow to his left cheek, cutting through his right eye and nose. His right eyelid seems to be closed permanently, and the skin is purplish-red and lumpy. His nose seems mostly intact, but the skin of his left cheek looks webby, like the results of a large, messy stitch-job. Besides the scar, he is quite handsome—his jaw strong and square, and his left eye dark brown and fiercely focused on you.

He looks at Mak, standing beside you, and says something you don't understand. Mak blinks and says nothing. The man repeats himself and Mak nods and says "*Ae*," which Mak had taught you meant "yes" in Hawaiian.

Then Mak turns to you and says, in a trembling voice, "He says he is the king here, and he wants to know if I can understand his language because I have tattoos like his men. I said I will translate for you—it's close enough to Hawaiian."

Turn to page 102.

102

Mak gulps, and you both look back at the king. He begins speaking in a steady, confident voice. Every so often he pauses and waits for Mak to translate to you. His speech, in Mak's words, went like this:

"Foolish people who have come to my island. You are standing in front your king. Do you see the treasures all around you? Do you see the ocean down below you? These are the symbols of my power. You will be my subjects, as long as you are alive.

"Yesterday a ship crashed onto my shore, just down the beach there. A big, beautiful ship with many men on board who wanted to trade with me. They wanted to trade spices—ha, flavored dust! These men were helpless—their ship was ruined, and they asked me for food, for shelter from the rain and wind. They wanted me to show them kindness. I asked, did they have any silver? They said no, they only had the spices—they were on their way to trade the spices for silver when they landed on my beach.

"Did they think I was so stupid? I have been tricked by men like that before. To be kind is feeble. To show mercy is a weakness. I gave them a meal, to calm them down. Then today I cut off every one of their heads. If you look out this other window, you can see them—the heads. I put them on the beach on those sticks so everyone sailing by knows exactly what will happen to them if they land their ship here: they will never leave."

Go on to the next page.

He stops talking and Mak finishes translating. Your legs feel like jelly and your stomach is cold with fear. The king watches you closely and then points out the window down the beach, inviting you to look. You take careful steps, not sure you want to see. Every few feet, for a hundred yards down the black sand, is a human head atop a ten-foot pole. Blood has pooled below.

The king speaks up again, and Mak translates:

"Who are you? Why are you here?"

You don't know what to say.

"Where did you come from? You are different from those other men. You wear different clothes. You do not look like sailors. Are there more of you?" His voice is louder now, but Mak remains calm, and you remain silent.

"Where is your ship?" The king shouts this last question. He is getting impatient.

You see the mountain out the window, too, over to your right, and you could have sworn that this beach right in front of you, with all the heads, is the beach that *Albatross III* crash landed on just last night. But it's nowhere to be seen. Farther down the beach, you see an enormous, multi-decked, timbered ship with beautiful, wide white sails and an ornate bow. It looks like a Spanish galleon, which you've seen pictures of in history books. The thing is, galleons haven't been in use since steamboats took over in the eighteenth century.

Turn to the next page.

104

Ever since those vibrations on the mountain, you've been suspecting that something really weird is going on. You're a scientist—you base your beliefs in facts. But these facts are adding up to a very unlikely conclusion: *you went back in time.*

You've read theories about magnetic fields causing wormholes through time, and you suspect that the mountain is a powerful magnetic source, especially if it is a volcano filled with a molten metal core. You have an idea.

"Mak, tell him that we have special powers," you say quietly.

Mak looks at you like you've grown another head.

"Just tell him. Tell him we are—I don't know—immortal. Not from this world. Tell him we can communicate with each other telepathically."

"I don't know if that's a good idea," Mak says.

"Do you have a better one?" you snap. "He's going to put our heads on stakes unless we do something to change his mind."

Go on to the next page.

Mak nods and speaks to the king. At Mak's words, the king's eyes widen. He is silent and looks back at you, studying your face for the truth. Then he says something back to Mak, who says to you, "He wants you to prove it."

"Okay, I have a radio in my pocket, and Andrea has the other one. This will work. Now translate for me." Mak nods, still looking uneasy. "First, ask him to untie my hands."

The king says something to a guard who cuts the rough rope that bound your wrists. The guard stays next to you, knife drawn.

"Thank you," you say and stretch your arms before reaching casually into your pocket and holding down the transmit button on your radio. Then you begin: "Your highness, thank you for allowing us to speak with you. I want to demonstrate our special abilities. I think you will be impressed. Our friend is still down in her prison cell, but I will communicate with her through my mind. All I have to do is think about it very hard, and she will hear my voice in her head. Now, I would like you to tell me how old you were when you got that scar on your face."

Mak freezes at these last words, and you're nervous too. You're pretty sure this is not a subject that the king discusses with just anyone, but you wager that the more personal your questions, the more he will trust you in the end. You nod at Mak in encouragement, and he relays your words.

Turn to the next page.

106

The king's eyes widen and he looks for a moment like he might explode with rage and cut off your head right now. But you can tell he's vain and power hungry, which makes him curious. He finally speaks to Mak in a low voice.

"I think he said seventeen," Mak says, "But I'm not positive."

"Ask him to draw it out, so we know for sure."

The king removes a small, silver knife from its mount on the wall, and approaches you. You gulp. Maybe you made a big mistake. Then he turns to Mak and puts one arm across his neck, pushes him against the wall, and brings the knife to his chest. He touches the tip to Mak's dirty t-shirt and drags it down a few inches. The blade is so sharp that it slices right through the fabric without tearing it. He does this sixteen more times. Mak is trembling and sweating, but he doesn't move. You count the tally twice to make sure and say to him, loudly, "seven—seventeen." And then, quieter, "I'm sorry, Mak. I didn't know he would do that."

But Mak is looking down—blood is seeping through a few of the cuts in his shirt. "It's okay," he says, seeing your shocked expression. "I'm fine. It's just a scratch. He wants us alive. He wants to know your secret."

Go on to the next page.

"Okay, seventeen," you say aloud again, willing your voice to remain strong and confident. "Seventeen. Seventeen." You close your eyes and pretend to be concentrating very hard. Then you open your eyes. "Now, if you send one of your men down to the prison, they will see that our friend has received my message, and there will be 17 lines drawn on the floor of her cell."

Turn to the next page.

108

As soon as Mak has finished translating, the king barks at one of the men standing by the door, and he leaves in a flash. You all wait for his return in silence. You stare at Mak, but he won't meet your eyes. You feel terrible, but you have to believe your plan will work. You have to believe that Andrea had her radio turned on and that she heard everything you just said during the last five minutes.

Just then the door flies open and Andrea walks in, her hands tied. Her hands are tied! Was she able to draw the lines at all? Or did they tie them just now, before transporting her to you? The guard speaks and Mak translates excitedly:

"He says he watched her draw the last lines when he opened the door. There were 17 in all."

The king is staring at Andrea as if she were a ghost. Then he looks at the guard and shouts something. The guard mumbles something else in reply.

"He's calling him a liar," Mak whispers.

You think maybe this isn't working in your favor after all. The door is open, and the king is distracted with his guard. You make eye contact with Mak and Andrea, and they look as unsure as you do. Maybe you should make a run for it.

If you decide to try to escape, turn to page 99.

If you think you're better off trying to stay in the king's favor, go on to page 109.

You wait. The king and his guard argue for another minute, and then they both turn to look at you with pale, frightened faces. Then the king does the unthinkable: he falls to his knees in front of you. Mak translates the king's slow, quiet words.

"I am sorry I imprisoned you. I did not recognize you in this form. I know now you must be immortals if you can do this kind of magic. Please forgive me. My home is your home. Just please do not hurt me or my family." He doesn't meet your eyes.

You realize how much power you hold in this moment. If he thinks you're immortal, you can do anything you want. You think about all of the people down below in the prison and wonder how many of them actually deserve to be there. You think about the poor sailors who were tricked by this man and killed, and whose heads are rotting in the sun on the beach right now. You, Mak, and Andrea could walk away from this horrible place and try to find whatever time portal you slipped through—at least then you might get back to the wreck of *Albatross III* in time for a rescue ship to find you. The three of you discuss your options. Mak and Andrea's opinions are split, so once again, you must cast the deciding vote.

If you go to the mountain to travel back to the future in the hopes of getting rescued, turn the next page.

If you stay and help the people escape from the rule of their terrible king, turn to page 111.

110

"Let's get out of here," you say. "We need to get back home, ASAP."

Mak tells the king that you all forgive him, but you expect him to be kinder to his people in the future. He says you will be leaving now, going back to where you came from. The king seems to accept this news. He doesn't get off his knees. He offers you his knife, and you take it just in case. And then you're on your way down the stairs, in disbelief that you're walking away this easily. You keep expecting the guards to come running after you, but no one does.

You thought that finding your way back up the mountain would be easy, but the path you followed before doesn't exist now. After several hours, you think you're at about the same elevation as when you went through the time portal. You feel a tremor in the ground a few times, but your surroundings don't change. The houses and cleared fields are still there below you. After a few more hours of wandering back and forth, you all sit down and take a break. You wish you had brought some food or water along, but you escaped in such a rush.

"This is useless," Mak says despondently.

"Come on, this is going to work," Andrea replies, patting him on the back. "We've made it this far. We'll find it. Trust me."

All three of you look at each other and smile, despite your situation. You're so grateful to have such good friends and to have them by your side right now. No matter what happens.

The End

"I can't walk away," you say. "Think about what we could do here. Think about the lives we could save and all the pain and suffering we can prevent. Let's not run away from this chance." They both nod in agreement. Your positive energy is contagious. You help the king to his feet, and he smiles too. "We're here to help," you say to him. "This is your second chance. Showing mercy and kindness isn't feeble like you said. Letting fear and anger drive your decisions is true weakness." After Mak translates this, the king smiles again and offers you the knife still in his hands. You put it back in its place on the wall, no longer a weapon but a decoration.

You don't want to take over from the king, since this island is not your home—you don't know the language or the customs or the history. Instead, you encourage him to be a more kind and compassionate leader, and to try to make life better for his people. He respects that even though you have such strong magic, you don't use it to gain power. You, Mak, and Andrea live in the village and learn to farm. The people are fun-loving and kind to you. Eventually, you realize that you've stopped wondering when you're going to leave and instead look forward to every day of your new life here.

Turn to the next page.

112

One day, a ship arrives at the island. You know the king has changed his ways for the most part, but all the same, you understand he would be wary of outsiders. You are relieved to find that some of the men on the ship speak English, and they're equally fascinated to find you on this island. You ask one of them what year it is.

"It's 1776! Remember this date–the colonies in North America just declared independence!"

"We're from America!" you say, in awe.

The sailor looks at you skeptically and asks, "How did you get here?"

You learn that this merchant ship was on its way from China to the colonies in South America, but their food supply had been contaminated. They are more than willing to trade some silver for food. With Mak translating, the king obliges. A festive meal is prepared for the hungry sailors, and that night, with all the food, music, and dancing, you have the most fun you think you've ever had in your life.

When the sailors leave the next day, part of you wants to go with them, but you know you won't be more at home anywhere else in the world in the year 1776. This is where you belong now.

Turn to the next page.

As soon as their ship is out of sight, you feel the ground rumble, and for a heart-stopping moment, you wonder if the volcano is active again. But before you can think another thought, the whole world around you vibrates into white mist and then rearranges itself in another way. You blink. You're on the beach, and Andrea and Mak are beside you. Only this time, the whole crew of *Albatross III* is with you, too! Something you did back in time must have triggered a butterfly effect to stop your ship-wreck from happening. Maybe you prevented the whole curse of Blood Island.

You and Mak and Andrea look at each other with huge smiles of disbelief. You all burst into laughter, and Glen, standing next to you, looks up from his clipboard in annoyance.

"Quiet," he says, in that nasally, patronizing voice you remember so well. "You're going to scare away the birds."

"Oh, Glen, I never thought I'd be so happy to see you," you say earnestly, but laughing, and you give him an enormous hug. He clutches his clip-board to his chest and looks at you with one eye-brow raised, wondering what sort of bizarre joke you're playing on him. The two of you never did like each other very much.

"Don't worry," you say, "I have a feeling we'll find the birds, and they'll be amazing. But while I'm thinking of it, can I book a chess game with you for the trip back? I've really been honing my strategies for long-term decision-making. I think you'll be impressed."

The End

ABOUT THE ARTIST

Illustrator: Gabhor Utomo was born in Indonesia. He moved to California to pursue his passion in art. He received his degree from Academy of Art University in San Francisco in Spring 2003. Since graduation, he's worked as a freelance illustrator and has illustrated a number of children's books. Gabhor lives with his wife, Dina, and his twin girls in Portland, Oregon.

ABOUT THE AUTHOR

Liz Windover grew up in small-town New England. She has traveled widely in the United States, Central and South America, Europe, and the Australian outback, finding adventure at every turn. Liz had one life-changing summer living off the grid in the middle of nowhere, which taught her the importance of thinking outside the box. On any given day, she can be found at home in Vermont enjoying good food, good music, and/or good books. Liz's favorite idea is that we are all made from the dust of exploded stars.

**For games, activities and other fun stuff,
or to write to Liz Windover,
visit us online at CYOA.com**

Look for other titles available now!

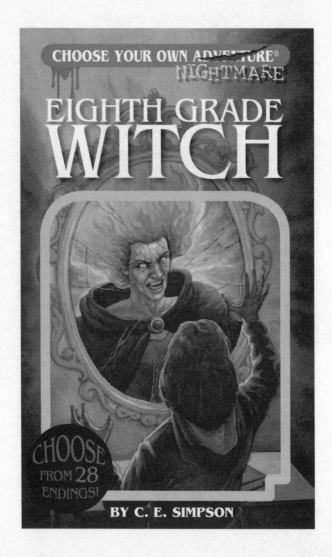

Look for other titles available now!

CHOOSE YOUR OWN ADVENTURE® 2

JOURNEY
UNDER THE SEA

CHOOSE FROM 42 ENDINGS

BY R. A. MONTGOMERY

Look for other titles available now!

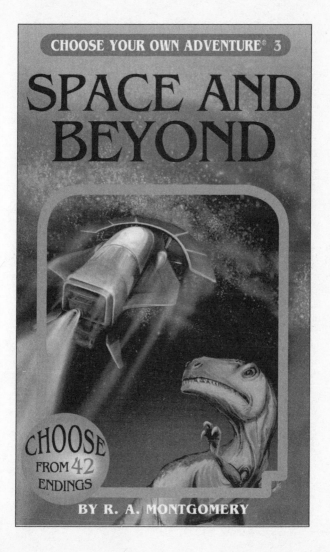

CHOOSE YOUR OWN ADVENTURE® 3

SPACE AND BEYOND

CHOOSE FROM 42 ENDINGS

BY R. A. MONTGOMERY

Look for other titles available now!

CHOOSE YOUR OWN ADVENTURE® 4

THE LOST JEWELS OF NABOOTI

CHOOSE FROM 38 ENDINGS!

BY R. A. MONTGOMERY

Look for other titles available now!

CHOOSE YOUR OWN ADVENTURE® 5

MYSTERY OF THE MAYA

CHOOSE FROM 39 ENDINGS!

BY R. A. MONTGOMERY

Look for other titles available now!

CHOOSE YOUR OWN ADVENTURE® 6

HOUSE OF DANGER

CHOOSE FROM 20 ENDINGS!

BY R. A. MONTGOMERY

Look for other titles available now!

Look for other titles available now!

Look for other titles available now!

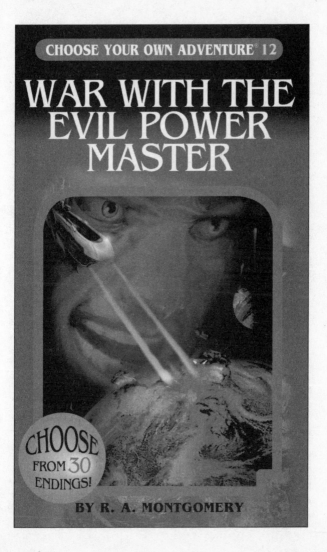

CHOOSE YOUR OWN ADVENTURE® 12

WAR WITH THE EVIL POWER MASTER

CHOOSE FROM 30 ENDINGS!

BY R. A. MONTGOMERY

Look for other titles available now!

CUP OF DEATH

BY SHANNON GILLIGAN

Look for other titles available now!

Look for other titles available now!

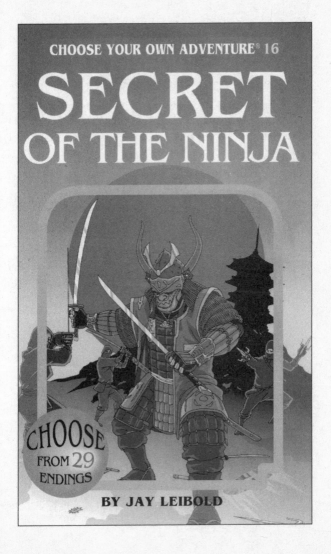

Look for other titles available now!

Look for other titles available now!

Look for other titles available now!

CHOOSE YOUR OWN ADVENTURE® 21

THE CLASSIC SERIES IS BACK!
CHOOSE FROM 13 POSSIBLE ENDINGS.

STRUGGLE DOWN UNDER

BY SHANNON GILLIGAN